Howling From The High Heavens

Poetic Pearls on the Path of Kundalini Kriya Yoga

Rudra Shivananda

Alight Publications

2022

Howling from the High Heavens

By Rudra Shivananda

First Edition Published in October 2022

Alight Publications
PO Box 277
Live Oak, CA 95953
http://www.alightbooks.com

Howling from the High Heavens © 2022 by Runbir Singh.

All rights reserved. No part of this publication may be reproduced, stored in a retrieval system or database, or transmitted in any form or by any means electronic, mechanical, photocopying, recording, or otherwise without the prior written approval of the author or publisher.

Softback ISBN: 978-1-931833-63-9

Printed in the United States of America

I bow to that resplendent Pearl
Hidden in the ocean negation
That Pearl no diver can reach
You cured my malady of duality
With Love's nectar of immortality

Table of Contents

1. Spirit Song / 7
2. The Warrior / 8
3. The Play of Time / 9
4. Refuge / 11
5. The Seeker / 12
6. What is Beautiful? / 13
7. The Mountain Path / 15
8. The Presence / 17
9. My Master / 19
10. Spiritual Evolution / 21
11. 84,000 Paths ! / 23
12. Wahe Guru / 24
13. Samadhi / 25
14. In Light of Kriya / 27
15. Moksha / 33
16. Live God-1 / 34
17. Live God-2 / 35
18. The Attributes of Self- Realization / 36
19. Beware Material Spiritualism / 40
20. The Meaning of Life / 41
21. No Regrets / 42
22. Beyond the Dream / 43
23. Life Lesson Learned / 44
24. A Polished Gem / 45

25. Awaken / 46
26. Prayer / 47
27. Motion in Stillness / 49
28. The True Wine / 51
29. Falling Rose / 53
30. My Wish / 54
31. Compassion / 55
32. The Practitioner / 57
33. That I am / 62
34. Freedom takes Effort / 63
35. Guru's Grace / 64
36. Howling from the High Heavens / 67
37. Yogi / 68
38. Stormy Seasons / 69
39. Acceptance / 77
40. Nothing in Everything / 79
41. True Self / 80
42. Play of Light / 85
43. Divine Mother / 87
44. The Pilgrims's Progress / 89
45. Awake to New Life / 95
46. Nature's Home / 98
47. Winter's Warning / 99
48. Voice of Victory / 102
49. My Real Home / 104
50. Perfection / 106

Spirit Song

Born with these mortal eyes,
truth be told I could not see
Trapped in my house of nine doors,
how happy could I be?
Seeking for the way that I cannot find
I yearn for that home
the one I left behind

To find that path,
I closed the doors and lost my sight
Piercing the darkness,
I embraced the guiding light
Perceiving my self imposed obstacles,
I cut those karmic strings

My heart immersed
in that soundless song
that song Spirit sings
I am satisfied

The Warrior

I am born to kill
Daily I resolve to kill
To kill all my faults
To uproot all my guilt

I bathe in the sacred pool
Wipe away all shame
Cleanse away all blame

In my Golden Temple I kneel
Before the altar of light I kneel

Daily I resolve to kill
To kill my ego self
To unite with my True Self

The Play of Time

When I was young
I set out to find the way
Following the light of knowledge
My mind shone bright
My path was in sight

At midday I was lost
Illusions clouded my vision
Unsure footsteps faltered
Until Master's light appeared
Then Darkness disappeared

In quiet solitude
Meditation absorbed
In Work self dissolved
Clouds disappear, clear sky appear
Fearless light shines forth

Refuge

I found a deserted island
in this endless ocean
Mooring my leaky boat
I rested on firm earth
Watching the setting sun
filled me with melancholy
The moon and stars ornamate the sky
and give me hope
Should I stay or
sail on into the unknown horizon?

The Seeker

Seek your radiant Self
Set forth now, find the Presence
That Master that shines bright over the world
Him that awakens your eternal light

Awakening to awareness
Day and night, selfing to Self
Merge in that Light that lights all lights

Meditate to purify monkey mind
Live purely to pacify desires
Live a loving life free from strive
Mindful in work and play

What is beautiful?

Divinity is beautiful
Righteousness is beautiful
Self-discipline is beautiful
Compassion is beautiful
Spiritual practice is beautiful
Self-realization is beautiful

Seek and strive for true beauty
Consciousness the only reality
Drop razzle dazzle flim flam fantasy
Your True Self is the real ecstasy

Rudra Shivananda

The Mountain Path

Plow the field,
pull the weeds and
remove hidden roots
Sow the seeds that will bear
the wish- fulfilling fruits

Day in, day out,
begin at the bottom
Up and down,
Climb the mountain path
Seeking Divinity at the peak
My True-Self I meet

The Presence

I take refuge in that auspicious Presence
Who removes the worldly bonds that bind us
That giver of true knowledge
Who removes our mayic ignorance

I take refuge in that auspicious Presence
Who is the embodiment of saving grace
That SatGurunath, the perfect guide
Who illuminates our inner precious polestar

I take refuge in that auspicious Presence
Who protects the seed of our essence
That Siddhanath, that pure path of perfection
Who grants us the gifts to pierce our limitations

I take refuge in that auspicious Presence
Who is beyond Divine Mind
That existed before the world manifest
Who skillfully dissolved my illusive ego

I take refuge in that auspicious Presence
Who protects us from our wayward senses
That Yogiraj, the seer that cures our blindness
Who leads us to abide in natural bliss

I take refuge in that auspicious Presence
Who wakes us from our dreams
That being beyond the states of becoming
Who shows us our true Self to Be

I take refuge in that auspicious Presence
Who is changeless in the states of body and mind
That being who wields the power of maya
Who liberates us from states of waking and dreams

My Master

Maya the mortal binds
Only a play the yogi finds
Death's claws sunk in mortal hearts
Immortal soma transformed by siddha arts

No holy institution for liberation
No dogma cage to bind nor fancy stage to pray
No ochre robes nor color strobes for meditation
No ego balm so in child's play do not stray

A thousand life-times of tears
My soul cry finally He hears
In darkness a light, Yogiraj appears
Liberating me from countless fears

True yogi needs no external tools
True yogi one's body the only school
True Guru the only guiding light
Ignorant ego forces to fight

Shiva-Shakti unparalled gift
Great Seal kundalini to lift
Five-pointed star to light the way
Cosmic hum leads home to stay

Rudra Shivananda

Sat-Gurunath Supreme
Wakes me from my dream
Drops drip from nectar well
Saves soul in karmic hell

Soul suffused bliss swell in third-eye sight
In the sky pouring life Surya Divine Light
On Earth Gurunath warrior's might
In my heart Babaji guiding light

Breathing through my breath
Thinking through my thoughts
In thy light I become aware
Thy grace saves me from karmic snare

Clear light of no mind
How rare to find!
Poetical verses I have none
Siddhanath you are my Sun.

Spiritual Evolution

What is Yoga?
State of Self-Realization
Pathway to Self-Realization
Process of Self-Realization
Union with the Divine
Shiva-Shakti
Soul-jiva to spirit-Atman
Super-consciousness: Samadhi
Divine Consciousness: Samadhi
Cosmic Consciousness: Samadhi
Liberation: Moksha
Freedom from Rebirth: Moksha
Freedom from Karma: Moksha
Enlightenment

84,000 Paths!

Why are there so many different yogas?
As many as there are types of people
Everyone in every life has a chance
to find the Divine Within
A yoga to suit each and every soul
No soul left behind, no soul forgotten.
Kriya Yoga
Hatha Yoga and Raja Yoga
Jnana Yoga
Tantra Mantra and Yantra
Kundalini Yoga
Bhakti Yoga and Karma Yoga
This life is precious
Death is inevitable
Departure time is unknown
Why waste energy on passing bhoga?
Start now the practice of yoga.

Wahe Guru

Shiva-Gorakhsha-Babaji
Gorakhshanatha
Gorakhnatha
Goraksha
Gorakh

Unborn
Undying
Lightning standing still
Eternal Youth of sixteen summers

Eternal Now
Ancient of Days
The Great Sacrifice
Babaji

The Light that lights the Light within us
Sanatana
Sat Nam Shri Wahe Guru

Samadhi

Samadhi happens only —
when mind disappears.
Why ask what happens?
What a joke!
Those who know speak not
Those who speak, know not

Samadhi happens only —
when mind disappears.
Beware the mind's cheap tricks,
snakes from sticks!
Sages compassionate words twisted.
Ego-mind false visions created.

Samadhi happens only —
when mind disappears.
Like tortoise body-sense still,
by concentrated breath, let mind still.
From the many to one to none.
From still mind to no-mind to self-effulgent Sun.

Rudra Shivananda

In the Light of Kriya

In light of Kriya absorbed
Reflections five appeared
Accumulated effects
Of my thoughts, words and deeds
No strangers these
Embodiment of my ignorant suffering
Adharmic born
Visible manifestations of my karmic bonds

My Eye in dharma abiding
Marveled at Maya's magical plays
Ever vigilant guide awakened
By the living Guru's grace
Golden-hued youth shows the way
To cross the ocean of samsara
The Ancient of Days in whose undying light
Timeless fog of ignorance lifted by his might

In unconditioned Samadhi Yoga
Untouched by dharma or karma
The Self-realized Yogi
A royal path of transformation shows
These spiritual crutches he knows
A slave's redemption our ego-souls demand

Though in truth eternal be told
Neither path nor transformation our spirit knows.

In a merry moment I was swept away
In the embracing arms of my Divine Mother
Lost in the beauty of her eyes
The caress of her many silken arms
Caught in the web of time, space and causality
I cry out to my Divine Guru
In complete surrender I touch the lotus feet
Of Him whom naught may be said.

An unsurpassable gift from his illuminating ray
Transcending the limits of many lives
The grace of blessed sadhana
The skillful means to spiritual evolution
To ease the disease of random mind
He said a suitable remedy we must find
Instruction in the alchemy of total transformation
From karma to dharma to halt this mad motion

Sage Patanjali in sutras profound
Has self-control the first stage made
Yama he has counseled
The creation of new negative karmic effects to stop
Each aspiring yogi, yama must practice

Only then his actions towards liberation leads
Niyama next for positive karmic merit
To turn the future tide towards the clear light

Through tapas strong Shiva pleasing
Kriya Kundalini Pranayam
Burns the slag of past evil Karmas
Exposes the Soul's Golden Splendor
The true yagna pleasing to the Divine
Devouring the unborn seeds
Of our past karmic transgressions
Of dharma's orderly fulfillment.

Swadhyaya the paramount study
One's true self as separate from the ego
Paramhansa Yogananda an analogy made
An illustration in modern terms
The iron filings of karma are attracted
Only where a magnet of the ego still exists
Seeds of past karma cannot germinate
When roasted in divine wisdom's fires

When we heed the God Essence within us
Seeking harmony in contentment
Surely this is Isvar Pranidhan,
Supreme act of ungrudging acceptance

Christ Jesus taught us to pray
That the Lord's will be done
Our free will choice to heed God's will
Is indeed the way, the tao of dharma

Suffering from transgressions of the Law arise
Ever present the great Comforter
BhaktiYoga to right the Karmic balance
The Dark Lord his devotees assured
Even he with the worst karma
Who ceaselessly meditates on Me
Quickly he loses the effects of his past bad karma
And attains perennial peace.

Fourfold Dharma Law sustains and upholds
The visible and invisible cosmos
From the tiniest quark to the mightiest quasar
Inherent nature rules
In awe we but glimpse the universal law
Which scientists the puzzle to unravel
To protect society we follow moral imperatives
Imprints on our souls.
Orderly fulfillment of the human dharma
In olden days life's stages followed
Sweet nectar the fruit of Svadharma realization
Life's perfect individual pattern

Howling From The High Heavens

Natural tendencies and in-born aptitudes
Race and physical characteristics
The reflections five the sum of past karmas
And the effects of threefold law.
Karma the engine which drives

The wheel of life and death
Bringing us back
Threefold karma we have discussed
The past karma conditioning the present
The unfolding drama is from karma
Sprouting into our current experience
Waiting in the hidden fertilizer of our minds
The seed karmas past and new.

Good news bears repeating
The yogic sages a three-fold remedy prescribed
Non-attachment to the fruits of action
Practice yama to stop new karma
Isvar Pranidhan for acceptance
Righteous living of karmic consequence
Sadhana to burn the seeds of unfulfilled karma
Transcending cause and effect.

Knowledge being the antidote to ignorance
Which is the root cause of suffering
Shankara says "When everything is known as Self,
Not even an atom as other
When knowledge of reality is realized
No fruits of past actions can exist
With the resolution of the five reflections
The dreamer awakes to dream no more.

Moksha

Free from death
Free from birth
Free from rebirth
Free from sorrow
Free from karma
Free from desire
Free from ignorance
Free from the finite
Free from evil
Being Pure
Being Self-Realized
Being Divine
Being Immortal
Being Perfect
Being Enlightened

Rudra Shivananda

Live God -1

No one is ever alone
God is always with us
God is always in us
See God, Hear God
Taste God, Smell God
Feel God – everywhere
At night in bed, as we sleep
God holds out hands
Every breath – God breathes
Through us and in us
God will never forsake us
In the dark, God is light
God is the light in the heart
Put aside the mind
Hear the pure heart
Resounding amen find
God is within and without
Turn towards God
Follow your inner voice
God speaks to you

Live God - 2

God speaks through you
Life is precious
No time for depression
No time for grief
No time for anger
Time only for
Love, light and joy
Forgive all your hurts
Forsake all your desires
God loves you
Love God, Live God

The Attributes of Self-Realization
(inspired by the Upanishads)

The seeker all desires under control
With deep respect the Master approaches
For that direct knowledge of the One Truth
That wisdom light of liberating Self

The divine Guide in grace gives good counsel
Abide in faith and highest devotion
Attain to Self in profound meditation
From soul-mind to Self to God Absolute

Within light effulgence of heart chakra
Discover that transcendent consciousness
In patience and perseverance aspire
Such blessed state to completely immerse

Purify mind, heart, thoughts and emotions
Renounce desires and discipline ego
Meditate on God without distraction
Liberation with Eternal unite

Howling From The High Heavens

Seated alone in comfort and quiet
Body and back, head and neck, straight to keep
Worldly thought and relationship renounce
Salute with devotion the teacher guide

With calm serenity in heart lotus
That without beginning, middle or end
Realize That One, of wisdom and bliss
Formless, glorious, one with creation

Creator, preserver and destroyer
Imperishable, all-power, all-life
All that is and all that ever shall be
All-love, all-joy, and the death of all-death

Within seven chakras Om meditate
Destroy limitations and ignorance

Know That Self in all and That all in Self
Gain light within, becoming one with God

To express self, Spirit evolved bodies
Each new life molded by old karmic deeds
Discard psycho-physical consciousness
Attain bliss of unity consciousness

From That is born life, mind and five senses
From That is born five great elements
From That is born all the worlds and all souls
Now remember: That thou art; Thou art That

Know That as the object of enjoyment
Know That is the subject, the enjoyer
Know That is the process of enjoyment
Realize That as freedom from bondage

I am independent of the three states
Witness, knower and pure consciousness
Pure, perfect, tranquil and immortal
Eternal, transcendent Shiva, am I

Subtler than the subtle, greater than the great
The universe of manifold forms
The timeless One of cosmic creation
Eternal, transcendent Shiva, am I

I am the doer with no hands or feet
I need no eyes to see, no ears to hear
I am formless and beyond mind and intellect
Immutable and pure consciousness

Howling From The High Heavens

Sunlight shines down on sparkling waves
Visible vapors rise and vanish into the haze
Clouds come together to cover the blue skies
Roaring rains rush down the seas on every side
Natures ebb and flow in sublime science reside

All knowledge and wisdom by Self reveal
Self, the revealer of Truth – Self, the Truth
Beyond good, evil, or mind creation
Indestructible, birth-less and formless

In sacred heart, Supreme Self realize
Free from existence and non-existence
Pure and perfect, free from two, three and five
That witness of all, the absolute One.

Beware Spiritual Materialism

Meditation leads to fleeting peace
Drugs lead to fleeting euphoria
Do not trust in fleeting states of mind

Attachment to impermanent states
Leads to increase of ego I-ness
Trust not in temporal states of mind

Cessation of passing peace and joy
Suffering destroys each mental toy
Do not trust in fleeting states of mind

Ever vigilant, strive for refuge divine
Ever constant, practice death of ego I-ness
Trust not in in temporal states of mind.

The Meaning of Life

Abandoning opinions
Letting go of virtue
Passing through knowledge
Seeking truth
Abiding in boundless peace

Find heaven on earth
Spirit within body-temple
Realize True-Self in self
Divinity within humanity

Seek not the meaning of life
Strive to realize the truth
Satisfy your life with meaning

No Regrets

Play not the game of karma judging
The results of karma are mysterious
Let us be serious, develop insight
Act now in good faith and conscience

Let there be no regrets
Neither guilt nor fear to appear
Each night surrender to Divinity's might
At Each dawn give thanks to new day

Beyond The Dream

Am I the dreamer
who dreams he is dreaming?
Am I the dreamer
who dreams he is awakened?
Awake, Aware,
Follow the Master's Light
Tread the path beyond
Divine dream's might

Rudra Shivananda

Life Lesson Learned

From afar
to here and now
winter's blow,
Death's dark and dreadful shadow
Ever shakes one's mortal coil
Rusty prayers from mumbling mouth
Deter not
Death's deadly arrow.

The material man
moans and mourns.
O Death, Wait, Wait,
it's not time yet.
I have made much in this sojourn
More, more, much more to be done yet
O Death's stern gaze dash hope forlorn

As greedy eyes grasp at worldly toys
wisdom's heart laughs
at fleeting joys
Bubbles in a stream,
stars lost at dawn's sight
A flickering lamp, passing rain, lightning flash
Dark Dreams disappear in wisdom's waking light

A Polished Gem

A sapphire in the rough to shine
Cut, facet, polish, brilliance reveal
Soul mired in mayic mud unreal
Burn karma
enlightenment to unveil

Awaken

Awaken, awaken now
Abandon dogma
Abandon words
Abandon speech
Abandon thoughts
Awaken to selfless bliss

When thought objects disappear
Where does thinking subject appear

Prayer

Worship not the false idol of
Ego-self
Inhale the incense of prayers
Om True-Self
Realize O divinity
with every breath
Exhale O fragrance of
universal love
Dissolve bondage,
merge O unity,
Om freedom

Motion in Stillness

Restrain the body and relax
Shut the mouth and stay silent
Empty the mind and think no thoughts
Cease to cling to perfect your practice
Be like the hollow bamboo and act in rest

Rudra Shivananda

Put no trust in words
Put no faith in thoughts
Rest where Being is
Not one or two
No yesterday
No tomorrow
Not even today

The True Wine

I want to drink the true wine
Wine that can be bought is not the true wine
Glass that breaks is not the true glass

What a shame to be sober
When you can be divinely drunk
Dream big or small
Live long or short
Life comes to an end
Drink from immortal stream
Let pass not wine sublime

Rudra Shivananda

Falling Rose

Grief
love loss
tears fall
Heroic heart helpless pall
Let go baseless blame
Let go silent shame
Let go gnawing guilt
Honor shining soul's flight
Cherish
shared joy's
delight

My Wish

I want to wake up
at home
Where freedom reigns supreme
Where no desires are unfulfilled
Where no karma is concealed
Where tears of time flow no more
Where love
unceasing floods and flows
I wish for the wonder of
peace and joy

Compassion

The truly enlightened
chooses compassion
There is
no personal liberation
when others suffer
Abandoning the duality of
bondage and liberation
Strive to
help all beings
overcome
the life-death cycle

The Practitioner

Relax the body, tension free
let it be
Lightly close eyes, breath deep
take three
Lips firmly seal,
silence remain
Empty mind, thoughts naught,
be free
Steady spine, Hollow reed,
prana wind to watch
Take naught, give naught,
grasping cease be
Holy words whispered cannot Realization reach
Light mind to
Divine Mind to
No-Mind
can reach
Constant practice,
detachment,
Satguru's grace beseech

Rudra Shivananda

Wishing for a good day
Generate goodwill today
Stretch out your hand
Smile, let not hate stand

Howling From The High Heavens

Wisdom's heart virtue's aim
Hopes and wishes reclaim
Right action ego-mind tame

At daybreak let the sunshine in
Harness will, Breathe prana within
Let love, light and joy begin

At dusky dark let moonbeams in
Control mind, suffuse nectar within
Let bliss and immortal life begin

Rudra Shivananda

Fantasy or reality, mind's polarity
Existence or illusion, mind's delusion
Nirvana or samsara, mind's duality

That I am

Realize and rest in your true nature
Abide in calm and clear consciousness
That neither rests nor moves
That neither becomes nor ceases to be
That neither comes nor goes
That neither affirms nor denies
That neither stays nor departs
That I am

Freedom takes Effort

Becoming
who we want to be
takes effort
Laziness and doubt
we must resist
Relying on Gurus grace
guidance surrendered
In precious practice
we must persist
Realizing true Self is
to be unfettered

Rudra Shivananda

Guru's Grace

Guru's grace awakens me
from illusion's dream
Guru's grace leads me
across samsar's stream
Guru's grace transforms me to
Hamsa supreme

Myriad salutations to
The Presence
beyond the mind sea
Eternal Master that
transforms myself to Self,
being to Be

The Presence
Enters fire without being burned
Goes into water without being drowned
Hells and heavens are merely festive fairs
Walks unharmed amongst phantoms and wild beasts
Our trivial tribulations are easily
resolved in the Presence

Howling from the High Heavens

Soul swan seeks to surpass humanity's sorrow
Raging river roars through birth and death
Lonely tree with falling leaves shade sun's embrace
The wanderer walks the earth to console the weary
Disease, decay and death destroys body temple
Why wait to howl to the high heavens at death's door
Waste not life's limit of five score years with regret
Listen and heed the ringing bell
Drink the divine sparkling wine
Sing soul's song and sound the victory conch
Surely to soar beyond, beyond the high heavens.

Yogi

Immovable and serene,
the yogi practices no virtues
Self-possessed and dispassionate,
the yogi commits no sin
Silent mind, subservient senses,
the yogi curbs all desires

Stormy Seasons

Sunlight shines down on sparkling waves
Visible vapors rise and vanish into the haze
Clouds come together to cover the blue skies
Roaring rains rush down the seas on every side
Natures ebb and flow in sublime science reside

Passion storms from vain clouds bind
Seasons play in restless mind display
Mind like a vast and boundless sky refine
Natures way with divine grace to stay

Fragrant flowers blooming in spring
Cool breeze under the summer sun
Harvest moon in autumn is awesome
Fires flame warms heart in frigid winter
We wish all the while for a second spring

Rudra Shivananda

In the ebb and flow of life,
how foolish to fight for gain
Without knowing one's self,
the learned compete for fame
What price ambition,
it is better to be simple and plain

No one has walked my road before
No one will walk this road again
Success and failure
a mere passing scene
Praise and blame
mere obstacles foreseen
Mine eyes firmly fixed
Mine True Self to restore

Wisdom's heart virtue's aim
Hopes and wishes reclaim
Right action ego-mind tame

Restrain that mischief mind
That dividing mind,
that scheming mind
Abide in the calm ocean of
natural being

Rudra Shivananda

In act and play,
put forth full effort
Intent and thoughts,
revel in ruling right
In contentment,
seek not position nor fame
In practice,
seek peace,
pacify mind
In perfection,
abide in non-practice

Transform to
transcend this and that
Destroy distinction to
cut root of mind
Rest in reality
beyond decay, disease and death

Discernment destroys delusion
Equanimity eradicates ego
Illumination incinerates ignorance

Ultimate understanding is unity
Supreme action is without attachment
Perfect accomplishment is Self-Realization

Rudra Shivananda

Let not fear turn your head
Let not fear close the eyes of your soul
Look at the light for Self to see
Love the light for Self to Be

As the lotus flower grows in mud
yet is not muddied
As the Hamsa swan
separates milk from water
As royal Janak is not tempted amid his palace finery
As the enlightened master writs large but
leaves no tracks
May we live a spiritual life
in this material world of maya

Rudra Shivananda

A dwindling flame in a hurricane
A flickering light in the night
Life's illusion might in true sight

At the end of the mortal road
where the red moon disappears
Where even dread dragons appear
Where the seas fall from the heavens
Where you fall into the endless deep
That is where you find the place you seek

Acceptance

To move forward we must first know where we are
To transcend we must first accept all that we are
Embrace the whole, no part to discard
From genitals to brain, from heart to spirit
Buddha ate and answered the call of nature
Holy saints accepted their lusts and cravings to move on
Great scholars make mistakes, tangled in confusion
Purification is not denial, it is acceptance and renewal
As the wheel turns on the dirt, stay in the center

Nothing in Everything

Shakyamuni Mahayogi
under the bodhi tree
Teaches all beings to be free
To see nothing in everything
And everything in nothing
To cross the boundless ocean of suffering
Build your boat of non-attachment
Stitch your sail from compassion
And harness the wind of skillful means
The light of clear mind destroys all ignorance
In no time you find the here is there

True Self

The state of Self Realization is
beyond thoughts and words
It rests on nothing
It depends on nothing

What process takes you nowhere and
yet everywhere?
With no effort yet attain enlightenment
Who watches the mind and
Destroys all distinctions?
Breaking no bondage yet attain liberation

Just as in space shape and color form
Yet is not tainted by black or white
From Self all things emerge
Yet is not stained by vice or virtue

Just as no darkness can hide sun's glowing sight
The Self's brilliant light pierces Maya's might

Howling From The High Heavens

We speak words to explain Self
It is the light that lights all lights
Yet it is beyond words
Beyond all material essence
Yet itcontains all things

Be still for self to be Self
Relax body and mind
Empty mind, think naught
Spine as a hollow bamboo
Neither giving nor taking
When mind clings to naught
Self appears

Knowledge alone cannot save you
Realization comes not from scriptures
A mind clinging even to a lofty goal
Can never find the lightless light
Rely on the practice that reveals reality
Experience Self to shatter all illusions

Abide in non-grasping
Let thoughts rise and fall
Like the ocean waves too
Let not doubt derail practice
Let not sloth stop your climb

Be ever ready when the guru appears
The tears of countless lifetimes disappear
By guru's grace you are born anew
By guru's blessings liberation is near
In your mind make it very clear

Remember all things in this world
Are meaningless
One action leads to another
Action to reaction
All things are seeds of destruction

To transcend duality is the right view
To conquer the mind is the royal path
Stillness in motion and action at rest
Is enlightenment
Practice without goal leads to perfection

Transient is this world,
like phantoms and dreams
Change is the only certainty
Substance but a mirage
You cannot rely on things
Neither on kith nor kin
Not on wealth or public adulation

Live a natural life
Meditate on your true nature
Cut the strings of lust and hatred
Manifest love and compassion
You Attain to the unattainable

Cut the tree root and leaves wither
Restrain the mind waves and reality appears
One lamplight dispels an age of darkness
The lightless light burns the veil of ignorance
Grasp this moment and drop all hesitation

Rudra Shivananda

Destroy all distinction
Drop all differentiation
Cut the root of monkey mind
Stare at the singularity
That leads to eternity

Abide in that natural state
Beyond acceptance and rejection
Without birth or death
Pure and unstained by appearances
All desires and ego are dissolved

Play of Light

Master had tea with me
Dawn's sunshine behind
Mystic ode, a rhythmic light
Sparkling sight, how can this be?
Motes of light, master's might

Everything has changed in one breath
That really is all there is to life and death

Divine Mother

Kundali shakti-ma
Awakened by Sat-guru's grace
Rise up to Shiva's embrace

Kundali shakti-ma
Light the fire in my lotus shrines
Burning karma along my spine

Kundali shakti-ma
Pour out the nectar wine
To make me to myself Divine

The Pilgrim's Progress

A rare human birth
Due to past life merit
It passes in vain
Due to uncontrolled desires
The billionaire's private yacht or jet
Due to karma play on maya mind
What price Musk's deluded deer
Or Bezos's bumbling bee

Wake up and remove envy of wealth
Open your eyes and reflect on
why you were given this life
Due to careless and sleeping mind
It passes in vain

Remove doubt and delusion
Remember this life's value
Resist desire's torment
Refuse death's untimely embrace
Recognize your immortal divinity

Preoccupied with worldly pursuits
Deluded by outer glitter and glamor
Giving up on the path of Self-realization
Forsaking the real gem but grasping after plastic glitter
Fallen into the clutches of death and crying bloody tears

Rise above superficial form
Spirit knows no race nor ethnicity
Karma exempts no religion
Karma treats the wealthy and poor alike
There are no outcastes in eternity

Follow not the rich
for their wealth
Worship not the priestly
for their position
Honor not the performer or the athlete
For their fame
Venerate not the philosopher or scientist
For their brain
Death makes all their efforts in vain
Seek those who have discarded the five vices
Ever absorbed in the Divine

The divine flame within each of us
Is One and the same
The same unstruck sound vibrates
Within each and every atom
Heed not the heresy of separation

Just as
The fragrance resides in the flower and
The reflection is in the mirror
The Divine is in our hearts

We need not seek the Divine in forests
Or the high mountain caves
The Divine does not hide in trees or heights
Spirit pervades all things and is not confined
Mired by maya we search endlessly outside
For the jewel in the lotus within us

The answer to our prayers is in our hearts
Withdraw your senses and mind
Awaken to Embrace the shining splendor
Open your heart and follow the eternal melody
Your soul star to merge with the One Spirit

O pilgrim,
Abandon external ritual and worship
Within the mind, perform the sacrament
Within the mind, burn the incense
Within the mind, perform the sacred fire-ceremony

Wave your lamplight in the inner sky
Sound the resounding conch of nada Om
Approach the throne at the thousand-petalled lotus
By Guru's grace, the unknowable is known
The undifferentiated is realized

In human love,
we tear down barriers to embrace our beloved
How much more should we, in Divine love?

The shameless mind is married to maya
Night and day, darting in all directions
Mind is trapped by the five senses
Grasping after passing pleasures
Yet it's hunger remain unsatisfied

Howling From The High Heavens

The cycle of birth and death
We have sown with our ego deeds
Justice in action and reaction
Grasp the divine guru's helping hand
before the end of the hourglass sand

Why drink nature's wine?
It's intoxication soon wears off
A drop of divine nectar has
Quenched lifetimes of thirst
Chains of suffering are sundered

Close the nine doors
Collect the scattered mind in the tenth
There is the path home
There chimes the everlasting melody
By guru's grace sounds Om

The pilgrim's path to Self
Is walked without feet
Seen without eyes
Hum heard without ears
Awareness without even mind

Anahad nada is the root of all knowledge
The door to salvation
It is the Nam that breaks maya's bonds
It is the Omkar that crosses the ocean of pain
The Shabad that opens the gate to Being

Within our inner sky is an inverted well
There a lamp burns without oil or wick
It burns brightly day and night
Blessed is one who sees this light
By the grace of the SatGuru

SatGuru has shown the way
Death has lost its sway
Past life karma wiped clean
Liberating light constantly seen
Création hum constant companion

Awake to New Life

Live a new life awakening
Drink deeply of divine nectar
Delight in truth enlightening
Abide In serenity and joy
upholding wisdom's scepter
The weight of the world
crushes countless dreams
Seek the lightless light to
destroy dark karmic web

Rudra Shivananda

Fragrant flowers blooming in spring
Cool breeze under the summer sun
Harvest moon in autumn is awesome
Fires flame warms heart in frigid winter
We wish all the while for a second spring

Passion storms from vain clouds bind
Seasons play in restless mind display
Mind like a vast and boundless sky refine
Natures way with divine grace to stay
Light of guiding star in heart enshrined
Follow that star to break bondage's sway

Howling From The High Heavens

Battling through countless cosmic cycles
Beyond an overflowing ocean of joyful tears
Boundless Being in solitude
seeking soulful stillness

Let not disappointment rouse hearts blame
Self-same soul yearning
soaring moth-like to flame
Let devotion kindle lightless light to claim
Loving freedom's fellowship to
push back the night

Fearful hart, darting mind
consumed in self strife
Countless breaths breathed in countless lives
Sound Freedom's conch to
blow past ages' stain
By guru's grace tranquil mind
breathless breath attain

Rudra Shivananda

Natures Home

The spring rain has passed by
Dancing water drops from tree leaves
The wind anoints my face with water
My heart opens to nature's rhythm
Singing now this earth is my home

Embrace hot day or cold night
Awake In pure awareness
Meditate night and day
Reclaim your birthright
Nectar moon, life sun, in one

Remember we come from One
Realize that we are always in One
Let us live our lives in the One
In time, we joyfully return to that One

Winter's Warning

My red rose blooms in glory
Will I warn of winter's wilt ?
Wise words to live my story
This world goes on without me
Will I go on without it?

Rudra Shivananda

Why must I keep bothering me?
Myself in me wanting to see
Just to know who I'm meant to be

Inner sound unstruck,
I heard
Boundless freedom bliss,
I feel
Silence of eternity,
I seek

Shakti Om
Shivo-ham
Hamsah Soham

Rudra Shivananda

Voice of Victory

The sceptic doubts
the revelation of reality
Mired in sensuality,
They perish in futility
The wise searches for
unity within duality
They rise in that
victory of immortality

Howling From The High Heavens

Rudra Shivananda

My Real Home

Yesterday I had a dream
A dream that I was meditating hard
By a flowing river, 'neath sylvan boughs
I was happy but grew tired and decided
To go home, to my dream home
Quickly bathing and dressed
With rapid footsteps I tread the forest track
I laughed and ran faster but suddenly,
The dream ended.

Finding myself in my real home
I awoke to my own True Self

How strange this shadow play
I was searching for Divinity by the river
Returning to my shadow home to stay
My real home appeared
While the dream home disappeared.

Perfection

Transcending duality,
warrior's path tread
Conquering mind,
that royal road ahead
beyond mind,
the practice of non-practice is
Perfection,
siddha supreme, it is said.
Seek SatGuru's grace for mortality to shed

Books by Rudra Shivananda

Chakra selfHealing by the Power of Om

Yoga of Purification and Transformation

Surya Yoga - Healing by Solar Power

Breathe Like Your Life Depends On It

In Light of Kriya Yoga

Healing Postures of the 18 Siddhas

Insight and Guidance for Spiritual Seekers

Practical Mantra Yoga

Breathe Better Live Longer

Nada: The Yoga of Inner Sound

Living A Spiritual Life In A Material World

Transformed by The Presence

website: www.rudrashivananda.com
blog: www.sanatanamitra.com
www.youtube.com/user/KriyaNathYogi

About the Author

Rudra Shivananda, a disciple of the Himalayan GrandMaster Yogiraj Gurunath Siddhanath, is dedicated to the service of humanity through the furthering of human awareness and spiritual evolution. He teaches that the only lasting way to bring happiness into one's life is by a consistent practice of awareness and transformation. He has developed healing programs utilizing the energy centers [Chakras] and Prana Energy techniques through breath.

Rudra Shivananda is committed to spreading the message of his Master: "Earth Peace through Self Peace". He teaches this message of World and Individual Peace through the practice of Kriya Yoga. As a student and teacher of yoga for more than 50 years, he is trained as an Acharya or Spiritual Preceptor in the Indian Nath Tradition, closely associated with the Siddha tradition. He lives in the San Francisco Bay area, and has given initiations and workshops in USA, Ireland, England, Japan, Spain, Brazil, Russia, Singapore, Malaysia, Hong Kong, India, Australia, Canada and Estonia.